A Load Of Old

SQUI

Keith Skipper

Published by Keith Skipper and Jim Baldwin Publishing, Fakenham.
Distributed to the Trade by Paper Klip, Fakenham.

ISBN 0 9509060 5 0

Typeset by Fakenham Photosetting Ltd
Reproduced by Colourplan and printed by Colourprint
Bound by Dickens Print Trade Finishers

A Product of Fakenham.

Dedicated to all BBC Radio Norfolk Dinnertime Show listeners – with special thanks to those who can write as well!

Study the past, if you would divine the future.... Confucius.

FOREWORD

I am not in the habit of rushing into print – apart from the odd editorial in the *Wanglingham Gazette* when I think the backbone of the country is in need of a bit of stiffening! (By the way, the average weekly readership is now 106·8, so we are climbing steadily.)

However, I responded with enthusiasm when invited by young Skipper to compose this foreword, as the book, quite apart from its wild, eccentric, and, at times, "near the knuckle" humour, also serves the admirable purpose of reminding those of us who are fortunate enough to inhabit this fair county of Norfolk of those local traditions that are fast disappearing down that same long lane the ubiquitous honeycart took some time ago.

The fact that this noble service has left many of our communities with scant alternative means of disposing of "effluent" – I think that's the euphemism used – is something of a scandal.

The many anecdotes and comments contained herein also serve to fight an essential rearguard action to preserve the rich fruitiness and amazing verbal spectrum of the Norfolk idiom against the real possibility of it being surrounded by the myrmidons of national media cliché; and all accomplished by use of those droll,

laconic slings and arrows of Icenian wit (to continue this appropriate military metaphor) that is so much part of our Norfolk heritage.

I feel sure that some direct ancestor of those characters featured in this collection was on hand with a succinct comment concerning the rape of our good Queen Boudicca and her daughters by the Roman invader some twenty centuries ago.

Indeed, such is the devious quality of our Norfolk humour that, born and bred as I was in the county, I am never absolutely sure whether or not I am sometimes the butt of certain ambiguous remarks let slip within my earshot by my own workforce and tenantry!

With such highly differing and colourful accounts of local life and lore as the honeycart tradition, a belly-button fluff competition – (my lady-wife Amelia has never had the pleasure of entering one of those – she seems quite keen!) – church and chapel chuckles – (our local rector, the Reverend Jason Plunkett, was sad it wasn't seen fit to include any of the humorous anecdotes he contributes to the *Wanglingham Gazette* under the heading "Graveyard Digs") – whither the privy?, and the contributions of many listeners to that excellent Radio Thing – I jest! – (Norfolk, of course), to which I am myself a modest contributor – I cannot doubt that this delightful memoir will promulgate – I looked that one up – laughter, nostalgia and general delight in all who cast an eye through its pages.

Not only those readers who are less gifted in intellect than I, less sensitive, shall we say, less enlightened, but also those in our society who aspire to these qualities – honest sons and daughters of toil though they may be, through no fault of their own – even these will reap many a happy moment from this harvest of humour.

Thank you,
Egbert Gladstone-Pyle,
Wanglingham Hall.

P.S. Bates, our butler, enjoyed it too!

- *The harvest team at Brampton Hall Farm, near Aylsham, in the late 1800s.*

(Picture provided by Flo Gubb, of Brampton.)

THE SQUIT BUG

"No man who has once heartily and wholly laughed can be altogether irreclaimably bad"
– Thomas Carlyle.

There's no denying Norfolk's fascination with squit.

It's a part of the natives' staple diet, and newcomers soon get to like it as well. It is one of the first words to break down suspicions and barriers when a stranger strolls into a village pub where the local dialect is still on tap.

What is "squit"? Just nonsense, light-hearted foolery. "He talk a load of old squit" is usually accompanied by a half-admiring smile and friendly nod towards the exponent. It may be rubbish, inconsequential chat to fill the time, but invariably it carries an entertaining edge.

In my book the kings of squit are the Norfolk yarn-tellers, old characters who hold court and dare you to suggest there is a flaw in their act. They often tell the same old stories, but they can always manage to make them sound fresh, especially when new, unsuspecting listeners join the audience.

"Go on, Charlie, tell 'em about that night you found a ferret in your bed . . . and how her next door got the wind up when you put it through her window." Charlie won't resist for long. Fill his pint mug, give him a nudge, chuckle in anticipation – and away he goes with the embroider's art.

The newcomer to Norfolk may have trouble keeping track at first, but there'll be plenty of repeats to improve his or her education.

A pub is the best setting for squit lessons, and "refresher" courses for those who think they've heard it all before, but experience suggests the commodity can be traced in several other areas as well.

I took it for granted thirty or so years

ago when I helped out on the farm at Beeston, near Dereham. A puny youngster more interested in "gittin his snowt itter a book" was an automatic target for the wise men of the fields.

"Go an' fetcher pearler dry worter ... bring yer how, weer a' gorn muckspreddin' ... that wyre nettin on the sosh keep rearn orff th' old hins ... how long's short bitter string? ... if yew smell them danylions yewll wee the bed! ... git me a left-handed hammer ... thass no good blarrin', we wotter propper rearn! ... dew yew wotter odd job? Rite, go an milk the bull, thass odd job!"

Squit among the haystacks. Take it in the right spirit, or suffer instant abuse. I never fully graduated to the Agricultural Academy of Squit, but I got enough "O" levels to sustain me in the classroom and on the Norfolk rounds ever since.

I often bump into some of my old tutors from the farm. They still give me stick, but I can see it coming now. Meet squit with squit.

• *A privy at Felthorpe. Not used now but still in good condition.*

Perhaps it isn't accepted in schools as much as it used to be. Even in my young days, some teachers confused squit with cheek. When one asked me to leave the grammar school classroom until I could be sensible, I duly went – and suggested I'd be back in twenty years' time. I've just finished the lines.

Squit got me out of several potentially nasty scrapes in the playground. I couldn't fight my way out of a fertiliser bag, but I could land a few telling blows on the funnybone. There's nothing so disarming as being confronted by a scrawny Norfolk lad pretending to be oblivious to all dangers and threats, and daring you to spoil his punchline.

When I started work on local newspapers in 1962, it soon became apparent that squit was alive and well right across the county. Light-hearted snippits still brighten up many a page dominated by the serious issues of Norfolk life.

It became a habit to supplement those stories culled from reporting rounds with eager reading of books and articles dedicated to the delights of our local dialect.

Harbert's News from Dumpton in the local weekly newspapers, and *The Boy John Letters* sent to the *Eastern Daily Press* between 1946 and 1958 by that marvellous character Sidney Grapes, remain high on my list of squit winners.

In saluting the work of Jonathan Mardle – alias Eric Fowler – I must mention his part in my finding a place alongside him on the local press. As my schooldays were drawing to an end – and English remained the only subject at which I could safely be said to be outstanding – Eric paid a visit to Hamond's Grammar School at Swaffham.

I didn't meet him on that occasion, but he had a chat with our headmaster, Major Besley, with a view to finding out who might be suitable candidates for local news-gathering.

Major Besley's "vision" put me out of my uncertainty when he said I ought to make overtures towards Redwell Street in Norwich. Seventeen years of full-time writing about Norfolk events, characters and places told me it was a good piece of advice.

Eric Fowler gave me plenty of encouragement, not least because we shared great passions for Norwich City Football Club and the Norfolk tongue. He was an amiable professor when it came to squit.

In 1949, he compiled *Broad Norfolk* from letters sent in by readers of the *Eastern Daily Press*. The first *Broad Norfolk* was published in 1893, made up of 125 letters sent to the paper on the Norfolk dialect. Harry Cozens-Hardy, who edited that booklet, prophesied the dialect would die out within a generation under the influence of the Board schools.

However, that 1949 avalanche told us the local dialect had survived a considerable number of influences – including standard BBC English – and the squit wagon was still rolling.

Eric Fowler met the demand for a third *Broad Norfolk* in 1973. He stressed that newcomers were as interested as the natives in the peculiar dialect of the province in which they had settled.

Sadly, I could savour only one radio chat with him before he died in 1981, but there was time to thank him for his enthusiasm and industry on behalf of all dialect-lovers. He smiled. "Keep you a'gowin bor". I never saw him again, but the *Jonathan Mardle* volumes on my shelves are constant reminders of a scholar who knew his squit.

It would be presumptuous to suggest this book is in any way a successor to the work of a man of his stature. Suffice to say his efforts helped inspire it.

In his 1949 volume, where he amiably declined to attempt the impossible and standardise Norfolk spelling, he classified first the letters dealing mainly with the local vocabulary, and then those giving examples of the distinctive Norfolk grammar and phraseology. Within each of these he introduced sub-headings, and put "Norfolk sayings" and "Norfolk stories" in separate sections. Birds' names and carpenters' tools had chapters of their own.

Norfolk stories came more into play in his *Broad Norfolk* of 1973. Just over a decade later, the demand Eric Fowler was anxious to meet is as strong as ever. I'm more interested in celebrating that fact than analysing it.

He knew the value of letters, and they've been my lifeblood since I started presenting the Dinnertime Show on BBC Radio Norfolk four years ago. They've convinced me that squit is safe for a good time yet.

I've sifted through thousands of listeners' letters and limericks in an attempt to catch the true flavour of squit. It may sound pompous, and even patronising to those who suggest the Norfolk dialect ought to disappear up its own loke, but I think there's scope here for local social historians to add to their more recent observations.

After all, it's not long ago when most Norfolk villages waited for the honeycart to empty pails in the little sheds down the garden. We chuckle, safe in the knowledge that such visits are fast becoming part of our folklore.

That "shud down the yard" has inspired countless Norfolk yarns, some of them too earthy for general consumption. But many are based on vivid memories of a family coming to terms with life before the mains.

Similarly, we laugh now at the thought of the old tin bath in front of the open fire on a Friday night, waiting to receive a flock of grubby children. Boil another kettle, wring out the flannel – and the last one in can make mud pies!

Other areas provoke a sad sense of loss. Village chapels, pubs and schools continue to close at an alarming rate. The memories and smiles can provide some consolation, but here the squit carries a tint of mourning. The same goes for radical changes on the farm.

Many Norfolk yarns in this volume are based on real events, although time may have embellished here and there. A good story gathers impact over the years – as old Charlie's full glass will testify.

There are a few chestnuts, still sweet after all that time, but I've followed a deliberate policy of giving preference to previously unpublished bits and pieces.

The number of letters about honeycarts and lavatories may say something significant about the local character, and I did feel obliged to give a "health warning" before reading out some of the more salacious items on the Dinnertime Show.

Even so, they prompted hardly a whisper of protest, a tribute to the humorous way in which they were compiled, as well as the generous spirit in which they were received at mealtimes.

It's not a firm rule – indeed, there are none in this little jungle of jocularity – but squit carries a more pungent flavour when coated in our local vernacular. True Norfolk squit, I reckon, demands a true Norfolk voice to put it over. As the proud owner of such, I relished the chance to give all these letters on airing on the wireless.

Reading them out loud is one thing; preparing them for publication and quiet digestion is another. There are obvious variations in style, according to the personal whim and feeling for words of the letter-writer. Some are bolder than others in the use of dialect, and I've remained true to the original in as many places as possible.

Remember, even Eric Fowler knew the folly of trying to standardise Norfolk spelling. I feel the variety adds to the fun. Two old boys working on the same farm thirty years ago taught me that a good yarn could be told in at least two different ways. No doubt, they'd have had different ideas about phonetics and flavour if pencil and paper had come out with the fourses!

I've included some letters presented in orthodox English, because, despite the obvious squit element, they don't need dialect to make a big impact. For example, the vagaries of belly-button fluff is a subject for universal debate.

The limericks liberally scattered

throughout the book are all home-grown and fresh. Radio Norfolk's Dinnertime listeners have always relished this format, especially when I've suggested local words and phrases to work into their efforts. Plenty of our villages have been immortalised in this way as well.

My conviction that squit will continue to be a source of amusement and cause for affection long beyond the end of this century is based on much more than simple sentiment, or a cussed Norfolk streak designed to fight overwhelming odds.

It may be diluted. It may be ridiculed by those who care little for such regional riches. Sadly, an accusing finger must be pointed at a few natives as well as newcomers who want no truck with "dewing different".

Even so, my privileged position as a collector of Norfolk whimsy, much of it with an earthy flavour, forces me to lean strongly towards the suggestion that it can survive the computer and video age.

The squit bug is contagious, and it'll hang about for as long as we encourage it. One of the best Norfolk yarns, from well over half-a-century ago, underlines the survival spirit.

Mr Howson, headmaster of Gresham's School, at Holt, was determined to eradicate the local dialect from his establishment. He thought he was well on the way to success ... One day, on entering the classroom, he found that tea, which was overdue, wasn't ready. He turned impatiently to one of his head boys.

"Have that bell rung!" he cried. The boy looked up rather sheepishly and replied: "No, sir, that hent – not yit that hent."

Proof, surely, that the feeling for squit will always leave culture far behind on the Norfolk honeycart.

A pregnant young Mum from Stoke Ferry
Had a craving for sipping sweet sherry.
When the baby arrived
He hiccupped and thrived . . .
But his nose was as red as a cherry.

Liz Witton (Fakenham)

- *Horse-power to the fore in this sugar-beet harvest.*

Clifford Temple

THE HONEYCART SONG

by Bobby Benton

I never ewsed ter get peard a lot fer what
I hatter do,
Down ter the topper yer garden, an' in an
owter the loo
No matter what the weather wuz, if that
shood blow a gearle
I wuz the wun whood cum along an'
empty owt yer pearle.

Chorus

Cors I ewsed ter dryve the honeycart, yew
mite remember me,
Cors arter Iyd bin yew cood go agin as
regglar as kin be.

Now I kin teller tearle or tew, Iyre dunnit
fer sevral years
Lyke the Sundy pearpers yewd cut itter
handy squares,

• *Bobby Benton.*

The EDP wuz theer ter read asyde the
wooden lid,
But when I went in I hed ter grin cors I
cood smell wotyer did.
Iye gotter tellyer this wun, that job had a
funny syde tew,
Lyke when I saw Mrs Wossnearme
runnin' orff ter the loo,
Sheed jest dashed up the garden with a
fearce lyke a rearjin bull,
Then she say: "Dunt go away, Iyre gotter
mearke shure thass full".
An' Hinry's door wuz wyde opin when I
went ter visit him,
Wi' trowsers rownd his ankels he sit
theer wi' a gret ole grin,
He say, "Cor blarst, yewre early boy, got
noffin else ter dew?"
I say: "Thass orrite, jest tearke yar tyme
an' Iyll cum back ter yew".

Chorus

They wunt orl on this lektric owt in the
sticks yew know
An I recorl a cowld dark nite I saw this
torch aglow,
As I wuz gorn up ter fetchit he wuz then
cummin down,
As we parst he say: "Wotcher mearte". I
say: "Gernite Mr Brown".
Cors owt theer in the country them
howses arnt harf spred abowt,
An sunhow I dunt know now I missed this
womun owt,
Nex' tyme I went rownd theer she corld
me a silly ole fewl,
I dint care. I say. "Look heer, yew shooder
dugger hole".
But I tryed ter pleeze mer customers, the
yung as well's the owld,
But they woont go owt in the dedder nite
ter sit theer in the cowld,
Country fook arnt sorft yer know, they
hev a resarve insted,
An' thass innits plearse fer en emarjency
cearse, and they keep it unner the bed.

Chorus

I stopped wun nite at the lokul jest ter
hevver drink,
Ole lanlord haller owt: "Cor, woss that
ruddy stink?"
Thass th'owld honeycart, that nite she
dint harf reek,
So I went owt ter look abowt ter fynd
sheed spunger leek.
I ewsed ter keep th'owld cart cleen, Iyd
even polish it,
I spooz yewre orl a' thinkin' thass jest a
looder squit.
Cors kids terday know noffin bowt me an
the honeycart,
If yew say wot took it away, they wunt
know wheer ter start.
Well, I hoop yer dint mynd me tellin yer
wot I ewsed ter dew,
Pullin' owt them gret owld pearles frum
under the three ber tew,
Cors I dunt dew that job ner moor, got
mer rerdundansy,
Thanks ter the blook wot invented the
flush . . . he even got ridder me.

Chorus

A randy young fellow called Hudd,
Did his courtin' in his father's shud,
A mousetrap brought a surprise,
And a tear to his eyes,
Cos his love life was nipped in the bud.

David Turner (Martham)

Dunt stop ter hev a mardle wi' Sonya,
She's a gal who kin whoolly git onya,
My hart, she's a rummen,
An' them searme wads keep a' cummen,
"He' yer got enni bacci onya enni onya?"

Rosemary Tooley (Itteringham)

● *The legend of Litcham . . . Wally Feeke and his honeycart. Picture taken by* Peter Rowe *and presented to me by* Litcham Historical Society.

HONEYCARTS

"Blow, winds, and crack your cheeks"
– King Lear.

"For this relief much thanks"
– Hamlet.

There are several names for it. The night-soil collection vehicle is the posh one. More down-to-earth descriptions include the violet wagon, the lavender cart, the perfumed garden on wheels ... and even the humdinger for one that had a bell round Long Stratton way.

The most popular title is the honeycart, and the memories piled up as soon as I asked for stories about this notorious carriage of convenience.

I like to think those Dinnertime delights on Radio Norfolk inspired the *Eastern Daily Press* to come out of the closet on January 4th, 1984. On the back page, a stirring literary breakthrough with the headline: "Breckland to scrap honeycart."

The first time, surely, such a label had been pinned on the old wagon in our local paper in a serious report. The story referred to over 100 homes in Breckland still using pail closets being given five years to scrap them. The district council said they were dropping their nightsoil collection in 1989, leaving householders to make alternative arrangements.

Another push towards respectability, and a place in local folklore, came with local entertainer Bobby Benton's hymn of praise, *The Honeycart Song*, proving you can get a hit out of the most basic of subjects.

Those searching for international acceptance pointed to Clive James' *Unreliable Memoirs*, and his early days in Australia. "From outside in the street there was rattling, banging and shouting as the full pan was loaded on to the dunny cart."

That reminded us not to claim the wagon as a purely Norfolk institution, although it was hard to resist the temptation to make bad jokes about what they used to do down under...

My trail really started at Litcham Post Office, and a series of action-packed letters from Richard Bailey. His father, Gordon, was a regular visitor to our family seat at Beeston, delivering the weekly groceries when I was a boy.

Richard has inherited both his father's store and his infectious sense of humour. No surprise, then, to receive a batch of stories about Litcham's legendary Wally Feeke and his honeycart escapades.

The first highlighted the dangers inherent in Wally's calling ... Mabel Riches, who gave permission for the story to be told, went down to the loo at the end of her row of cottages one night, torch in hand. She was sitting peacefully when all of a sudden ... "Bang! Crash! Screetch! Rattle! The bludder thing's nearly full!"

Mabel shot up into the air screaming.

• *"Muster bin suffin' I et!"*

She ran home in a highly distressed state, her knickers round her ankles. There was a trapdoor at the back, and the luckless Wally had emptied the pail while Mabel was still busy above.

On another memorable evening, Wally was going about his duties along Back Street, opposite Lenny Allison's fish and chip shop. Jinks Fulcher and a few more Litcham lads were tucking into their chips and washing them down with Vimto when they noticed Ray Hooks, the bread roundsman, leaving his house.

As Ray passed Wally's cart, he closed the large door into which Wally emptied his pails. Wally reappeared from the house next door, and automatically hurled the contents "into" the cart without looking. He was smothered, providing his audience with a choking experience ... but then carried on as if nothing had happened. (For some reason, Wally never had to wait for service in the fish and chip shop – even when it was full.)

Wally Feeke's widow, the delightful May, recalled how in snowy weather, the only way he could make progress was to place sacks in front of the horse and cart. The expeditions took twice as long, and there were times when he got days behind the calls of nature. Wally hated bad weather.

May also reminded us of Wally's catch-phrase: "Sit yew still my bewty an finish ... Iyll cum back inner minnit". Pity he forgot about Mabel Riches.

Then there was the famous night Wally's honeycart was hijacked. Again, he was busy patrolling Back Street. While he was away from the cart, two American servicemen stationed at Beeston jumped on his chariot and charged up the Lexham Road at full gallop. It didn't take them long to get to Lexham on a mission designed to stretch USA–Litcham relations.

An hour later, they returned with more than a whiff of scandal. They'd travelled at such a rate, the movements of the cart's contents had forced open the lid. The

American hijackers were soaked, and unlikely to charm any young ladies that night.

Wally didn't ring up the White House. He simply scowled: "That'll larn them bludder Yanks!"

One more Litcham tale from old friend Norman Wagg, who remembers Wally with great affection, along with a host of other local characters who gave village life such a durable charm.

Wally used to own a meadow up the Tittleshall Road, and on this blessed plot he emptied the contents of his cart in a man-made pit. In winter, this pit would freeze over and form a perfect skating and sliding rink, Norman's favourite spot for getting rid of all that youthful energy.

One day, Norman and his mates were going full pelt, probably practising for the Winter Olympics on Beeston Lillypits. Suddenly, poor Norman made a cracking exit with a considerable splash. There he was, chest high in it.

It was one hell of a job for our frantic hero to clamber from icy danger, because when the pit was dug out, all the soil was heaped around the edge, giving extremely high sides.

Norman made it, emerging like a creature from another planet, dripping and smelling all the way home. What delights were in store? "I got a master's ding of the lug, boy, and a good thacking as well!"

So many Litcham adventures coloured by Wally Feeke's honeycart. May came into Radio Norfolk to share a few more chuckles, and Litcham Historical Society asked her to present me with that famous picture of her Wally getting on with a job that had so many others turning up their noses. The picture has pride of place above my study door – even though it isn't quite the smallest room in the house.

Wally's escapades prompted many listeners to go "beyond the pail". Mary Lambert, of Besthorpe, near Attleborough, turned to poetry in motion as she mused over the end of an era. . . .

The Passing of our Honeycart

Today, in our paper, oh Keith, did you see
Our dear old honeycart will soon cease to be?
The end of an era – a friend, trusted and true,
Without it around, tell me, what will they do?
We won't see our honeycart ever again
When these one or two people go on the main.
The tears in their eyes will appear with a rush
As they exchange their bucket for a chain and a flush.
Our river in winter's certain to flood,
But we always know it's water and mud.
With no honeycart to empty the load
I shudder to think what will be in our road.
But if they're in a muddle, I know what I'll do . . .
I'll invite them all over to borrow our loo.

Just what friends are for as the wind of change blows through Norfolk.

Robert Burrows, a lorry driver from Weasenham, was reminded of something he saw in Great Dunham some years ago:

"I actually smelt it before I saw it. I came round the corner and saw this Mini right behind the honeycart. It had run slap-bang into the trough they emptied the buckets into, and the previously full cart had deposited the load on top and all over the Mini. About fifty yards up-wind was a copper taking drivers' details. . . ."

We must not forget the dangers lurking for innocent maidens on holiday. Kath Bygrave, of Hethersett, recalled a holiday at a beach bungalow at Waxham when she was sweet sixteen:

"There was a pail closet round the back, but I had no knowledge of the existence of nightsoil men as father always used to dig the contents of our petty into the potato patch. (The old King Edwards had some flavour in those days!)

"After a midnight bathe in my one-piece

costume, I called in at the closet and removed my costume completely, not considering it necessary to bolt the door at that time of night. But the door suddenly opened, and this man and I stood staring at each other. However, he was a perfect gentleman. He said, 'Sorry, ma'am!' and withdrew, closing the door. When I emerged he was nowhere to be seen, and I learned from my friends about the night-soil men. He was so tactful, he didn't return with his horse and cart until I was safely in bed."

Gladys Lowe of Sprowston, had a similar experience on holiday at Hemsby as she tried to escape from the washing-up chores in the family's holiday bungalow. She was nicely settled with her book when the latch went on the door.

"I shouted, 'You'll have to wait a minute!' thinking it was just one of the family. 'It's all right, madam, we'll wait all day if we have to' came the reply. Yes, it was the rosecart man. You should have heard the family laughing."

Ron Hill, of Old Costessey, joined in the honeycart saga, but brought a variation to the theme. He was posted to India in 1943, and, with a handful of colleagues, had to open up an RAF station. One of the necessities – a honeycart:

"We obtained a tank, about 250 gallons capacity, mounted it on large iron wheels and built shafts for two water-buffaloes to pull. This duly went into service, complete with a very proud Indian driver. The iron wheels gave good warning of his approach – long before the smell arrived. The contraption successfully emptied many Elsans before it went out of use. Initially, it was called the Elsan Neddy, but it gradually became known as the Nelson Eddy.

"I don't think it could sing, but it could certainly hum. We never did see Jeanette McDonald."

When I'm calling phew....

The most popular yarn to surface down the honeycart trail was the tasty one about the two chaps busy on their rounds.

As it was warm, one took off his jacket and hung it on the back of the cart. A few minutes later, he noticed it'd fallen in. He tried to rescue it. His pal, a friendly type, said; "That oont be lotter cop arter that lot." Back came the reply, "I arnt consarned bowt the jacket, ole partner. I'm arter the sanwidjes in m' pockit!"

LATE NEWSFLUSH ... Another Norfolk honeycart, this one of the mechanical variety, was hijacked at Thetford by soldiers from a local camp. Len Howell was the Thetford Borough Surveyor and Sanitary Inspector who, on that fateful night in 1940, had to travel eight miles to find the vehicle and bring it back. Not so much a Thetford Chase – more a careful ride home from the Diss direction!

What was this fatal fascination servicemen had for honeycarts made in Norfolk? Perhaps it made a pleasant change from doing the rounds in jeeps.

"I hent harf got the gut-eark" said Dan,
"Since my missus got her health food plan.
I had ruffage, like hay,
For my fourses today,
And my short cearkes are ten per-cent bran."

Margaret Loose (Blakeney)

"Wotcher Fred, me ole partner" said Ted,
"I hope yar ole woman's abed."
"Yiss, an' I hetta nass'er"
Say Fred, "She's no wasser...
But me? Well, I'm bloomin' nigh dead!"

Ivy West (Corpusty)

• *Strolling home at Filby after a hard day.*

Clifford Temple

DOWN THE YARD

"Small rooms and dwellings discipline the mind, large ones weaken it"
– Leonardo de Vinci.

If honeycart tales were quick to surface, yarns about the "shud down the yard" simply flooded in.

Of course, there's a natural link between the men who came to empty the pails and those who did their best to earn them a productivity bonus. Indeed, a strong brand of camaradarie was fashioned over the years, especially in those rural areas where big families greeted the arrival of the honeycart with obvious relief.

You can stick what label you like on the old outside toilet. Privy, petty, the chapel of ease, the throne room, the thunder box, thc littlc housc, thc pail closet, the bucket shop, palace of varieties . . . virtually every

• *Just the place for a good read.*

household had its own name for that highly-important little building.

All of them far more imaginative and colourful than the blunt "bog" so prevalent today.

Many an outside toilet was given the camouflage treatment, tucked away behind privet, ivy or lavender. One of life's essentials didn't have to be too obvious.

In many cases, it was quite an adventure just getting to the place on a dark night in the middle of winter, torchlight dancing on the snow as you edged past the sprouts and cabbages. And what a delight to find no paper on the wall as you prepared for the trek back to the fireside...

Tearing up squares of newspaper to impale on the nail was one of my earlier regular jobs, and I often chuckle at the impish gods who decreed I should spend 17 years on the local press, providing fodder for fish and chip shops and for those who still hastened to the shud down the yard. How many of my reports finished up at the bottom of the bucket?

More sophisticated material has taken over, but that brings its own problems. There's not much to read on pink paper with little perforations, and one old boy who used Gordon Bailey's shop at Litcham insisted on asking for a "cupple o' rowlser Anthrax!" I'm sure he missed the delicate touch of the *Dereham and Fakenham Times*.

A vivid picture of what it meant to go on childhood safari in Gressenhall on a cold, winter's night was painted by Maggie Payne, of Norwich:

"We'd be sitting by the fire, listening to Dick Barton on the wireless, when you'd get the urge to pay a visit. First, you had to pluck up courage to ask someone to go with you. There'd be moans and groans, with shouts of 'Not again!' and 'I came with you last time!'

"Often you'd end up going on your own. I remember being so frightened but ashamed to admit it, and would venture out in the black unknown. Behind the loo we had a plum tree, and if the wind was blowing just slightly, the branches would tap, tap on the corrugated roof. The hurricane lantern standing on the floor would almost blow out, and nine times out of ten you never finished what you were in there for . . .

"Many's the time I've shot out, with my knickers round my ankles, heart pounding, breath coming in little short pants, tearing back to the house trying to compose myself inside ten seconds. When you walked back into the kitchen, everyone sat totally unaware of the terrible ordeal you'd just gone through. To think this went on all my childhood – I marvel I ever became an adult!"

Terrors recalled by Maggie Payne, but David Turner, Martham's master of whimsy, pointed out that the "shed with the peculiar chimney coming out of the side" could be a place of sanctuary.

"Whenever aunts and uncles and the like came visiting, it was the perfect place to seek refuge. Also, if you'd lost an argument or been told off, you can rush to the

• *New use for an old building at Thurgarton!*

bottom of the garden and wait for revenge.

"Sooner or later, your opponents would have to pay a visit, and you would holler out as they tried the door: 'Yewll hatter weart. I hent dun yit!' Smile as you heard them muttering and swearing to themselves, pacing up and down in the cold."

Sounds like a nice boy. Bungay had a few little devils as well when it came to getting into the local cinema without spending a penny.

Christine Ecclestone heard about the boys who opened the small door at the back of the old-fashioned toilets, removed the bucket and climbed up through the toilet seat into the cinema. Let's hope they replaced the bucket.

There were plenty of schoolboy escapades to add to the memories. Kingy Fowler, of Sprowston, wrote on behalf of a woman still laughing about an incident at the old Sprowston School before the First World War.

"The rear of the girls' dry toilets were approached from the boys' playground, and on occasions the lads used to get stinging-nettles and sting the girls' bottoms. One day, the headmistress was a victim of this treatment, and she reported the matter to the head master, Mr Tom Delves. No boy owned up, so all the boys in the class got six of the best."

Was it worth it? And did he sting them across the backside just to prove there was no preferential treatment in his school?

Former policeman Ted Beales, of Docking, had several tales to tell, opening his pocket book at Dersingham. "This boy waited until his brother Fred was well seated before quietly opening the door at the rear and pushing a stick through. This resulted in Fred rushing out with his trousers down, shouting: 'There's a bludder rat in here!' By the way, Fred, on becoming a man, held a situation of highest esteem."

I bet he gave his brother some stick when he found out it wasn't a rat.

Ted Beales then transferred us to Docking Police Station well over 40 years ago, when he joined the Norfolk Constabulary: "The sergeant would come in on a Sunday night before the magistrates' court the next day with an old *News of the World* which I would have to cut into squares.

"There was a sign on each toilet, one marked 'MEN' and the other 'WOMEN'. When the station was repainted, the decoraters painted the signs 'LADIES' and 'GENTS'. The sergeant didn't approve, and told them to do them again, stating bluntly, 'There are no ladies or gents come to our court.'

"The lavatory in the magistrates' retiring room was also a pail one, but considered very up-to-date. At the top was a hopper filled with cinder ash, and after the lavatory had been used, the user would pull a lever and the cinder muck did the necessary."

The wonders of modern technology at Docking, and I'd like to add "retiring room" to the list of names for that important little place. Another delightful slice of privy life with a police flavour came from

• *Typical little Norfolk house at bottom of the garden.*

"Wilson", of West Tofts, who'd asked a policeman for the funniest incident to come his way:

"One day he was called to a house where a very fat lady had sat down heavily on the toilet. One side, the bakerlite seat had split, pinching, cutting and trapping a slice of the woman's ample behind."

The seaside comic postcard scenario continues: "The small and worried husband was unable to help because the woman couldn't get up. She was yelling in agony, and hardly caring what the policeman saw. There wasn't much room, and after an almighty struggle, the policeman managed to take the back of the lavatory seat to pieces, thus allowing the woman to stand up with half the seat still attached to her rear.

"Policeman and husband set about prising open the split in the seat, freeing the fat woman completely. She went to the nearby doctor's for treatment. Next day, the policeman called again to take down particulars for his pocket book report. On seeing the officer face to face, the poor woman was so embarrassed."

Easy to laugh, but just imagine how she felt. And think what a fuss the same sort of incident would provoke today. Sirens, flashing lights, walkie-talkies ... the whole of Norfolk would know!

Grandmother's loo, discreetly screened by a tall privet hedge, was brought our way by Ivy West, of Corpusty: "Granny kept it spotless with a scrub-brush and a bar of Sunlight soap. There were two seats of office, the smaller one with a platform for little feet that couldn't reach the petty floor."

However, no-one was tempted to stay for a good read: "Granny had seen to that, albeit unwittingly, for in the corner behind the door were stacked a huge pile of books all in the French language – and identical at that. She'd bought them cheaply for that certain purpose from a local auction, and triumphantly borne them home on grandfather's wheelbarrow."

More two-holers came to the fore. Muriel Smart, of King's Lynn, told how she lived in a little bungalow attached to a chapel during the war. "We shared the lavatory with the chapel, and one day the visiting minister found my four-year-old daughter enthroned. 'You can come in,' she said. 'There is a big seat as well as my little one.'" Suffer the little children . . .

The Boy Derek John Ream, of Hethersett, broke into verse after relating personal experiences from his days on the farm where the closet was next to the bullock yard.

"This was one of the cesspit type, which got emptied once or twice a year with what we called a 'jet' – sort of a large hand-cup on a long handle. In hot weather, one would feel blue-bottles and horseflies brushing against one's hind-quarters, all the time hoping it wasn't a wasp!"

Here's the Boy Derek John's poem with a sting in the tale:

I'll relate to you, a little ditty,
Of old Charlie, who came from the city.
He'd never tasted country life.
Sad to say, he'd left his wife.

He was met at the station by a pony and
  trap,
A crate of chickens was placed on his lap.
They arrived at a cottage at the end of a
  loke,
Ol' Charley was thinkin' this int much
  a-ra joke.

And old lady came out, she say; come yew
  in,
And as he did so, out strutted a hin.
She say; I'm a-gorn t' look arter yew,
So I're med a noice onion an' dumplin'
  stew.

Ol' Charley ate up, an' said; that wor fine,
Then they finished it orf wi' hoss-radish
wine.
He set thar a-thinkin', how could life be
so humble,
When all a-ra sudden – suffin' started t'
rumble.

It wor plain that Charley would soon
hatta goo,
So he say; now m'dear, whereabouts is
yar "loo"?
I don't think th' ol' dear a-ever heard of a
"W.C."
But th' "petty" s'down bottom o' garden it
be.

Now old Charley looked down at an old
wooden seat,
Wi' about an inch gap, where the boards
didn't meet.
As he eased hissel' down – that wor a
bit-a ra "hum"
A blum'un "hoss-fly" – nipped him right
on the bum.

He wor hully "relieved" t' git out o' thet
plearse,
An' he went back a-gen, wi' smoiles on his
fearce.
An' he say t' th' mawtha, d'ya know m' ol'
dear –
I think I'll stay f' a bit – thas bew'aful
here;

"Ch-e-e-ri-O"

"Yewre orl on the huh, yew sorft pup",
Said pa when the hols. snaps tarned up,
Blarred sonny, "Tent me sir,
There's the Tower of Pisa,
Yew've streartned the ruddy thing up!"

Ron Starling (Sutton)

Someone getting hold of the wrong end of the stick is always good for a laugh, and several listeners sent in the yarn about the young married couple who looked over a house in Norfolk. When they got home, they suddenly remembered they hadn't seen the WC, so they dropped a line to the local vicar, asking if he knew where it was. The vicar thought WC stood for Wesleyan Chapel, and so he sent the following reply:

"I regret to inform you that the nearest WC in this area is five miles away. This is very unfortunate if you are in the habit of going regularly. However, it may interest you to know that many people take their lunch with them and make a day of it.

"By the way, it's built to hold a thousand people, and it has been decided to replace the wooden seats with plush ones to ensure comfort, especially for any who have to wait for a long time for proceedings to begin. Those who can spare the time walk, others go by train to get there in time.

"I myself never go. There are special facilities for the ladies, presided over by the minister who gives them all the help he can. The children sit and sing during the proceedings.

"The last time my wife went, she had to stand all the time.

"Trusting this letter will be helpful, and hoping you will be able to go regularly.

Yours faithfully,

Rev. W. C. Philpot.

"P.S. You will find the hymn sheets behind the door."

Finally to give this subject the privy seal, I asked for ideas as to what sort of books make good reading in the little shud. Suggestions included *Much Ado About Nothing*, *The French Loo-tenant's Woman*, *Chitty-Chitty, Bang-Bang*, *Wind in the Willows*, *Great Expectations*, *Far From The Madding Crowd*, *The Trumpet Major*, *Pickwick Papers*, *Winnie The Pooh*, and anything published by Pan.

• *Farming scene at Bedingfield in 1901, taken by the Rev. Thornton Shaw.*

FARMYARD TALES

"Here's success to the bright ploughshare and may it never rust"
– traditional rural toast.

I've paid tribute already to The Agricultural Academy of Squit, that earthy elite who saw my weaknesses as a farmworker about 30 years ago – and probed them so effectively it still makes me blush to recall their subtle advice.

My father and two elder brothers often joined in the chorus of rural abuse as the tractor clutch slipped, and the men loading the harvest on the trailer behind lurched and yelled, and threatened to cut off my supply of Woodbines if they survived.

They threatened to cut of something else when my version of the Harvest Field Grand Prix on the Beeston Circuit up Red Barn Hill trimmed out one corner of a stack being built so carefully. I simply misjudged the route to the elevator. I ate my fourses alone. Without beer. Just when I thought they had accepted me.

Despite my sad shortcomings as a holiday helper on the farm, I had to admire men like John Dawson, Bob Hall, Fred Burrell, Alec Wales, Alfie Hall and Charlie Powley.

Charlie was a thatcher supreme, and I can see him now, biking home for tea with his handiwork emerging like a strawed temple behind him. Harvest's crowning glory in the setting sun.

There was another lively congregation on the farm at threshing time, with its noise and muck attacking ears and eyes, while the dogs scuttled around following their noses. I kept my distance when the rats were goaded out of hiding, and I still go cold when I see one. Can't stand geese either.

Perhaps you can understand now why I was never fully accepted by the hard-working agricultural community. They put up with me, mainly because they knew I was going back to school soon, or – and this prompted wild celebrations behind my back – had landed a pen-pushing job miles from their fields of wheat, barley and sugar-beet.

How I savoured those final sessions in the summer of 1962. I shared their relief, even though I knew it was merely a case of being way ahead of my time in farming methods. Their jokes and yarns reflected the fondness of their farewells. "Weer gorter miss yew ... bludder pitty yew dint miss that stack!"

I'd picked up several handy words and phrases to help with the sort of sex education you had to learn as you went along. Listening to the men, and watching the animals, was better than any encyclopedia, and I swear it was never as embarrassing as many well-meaning people suggested it ought to be.

There are all sorts of romantic notions about being close to nature, early-morning ping of milk in pail, various answers lying in the soil. But I'm convinced the majority of country people do have a more healthy and open attitude towards "taboo" subjects like sex. And they see nothing wrong in a good chuckle when they're talking about it.

Could it be that several of their number have literally taken the bull by the horns and led him to bovine delights? Didn't we have some idea what would happen when we paid thrippence to take our doe rabbit to a neighbour's foot-stamping buck?

I make these points to prepare the ground for an earthy batch of farmyard stories sent in by Dinnertime Show listeners. They provided a natural follow-up, it seemed, to the honeycart and shud-down-the-yard yarns.

Some of them have been in circulation since the four-crop rotation began, but I defy you not to smile at any of them. (And you wouldn't have ventured this far if you didn't have a sense of humour.)

Jenny, of Costessey, set the tone with her tantalising double-bill. The first tells how a man strolled up to a farmhouse and tapped on the door. When the farmer came to the door, the man said: "I really am sorry, old chap, but I've just run over your cockerel, and I would like to replace it."

The farmer scratched his head: "Well, I dunt know how yewll mearke owt, but the hins are rownd the back!"

Then there were two farmers chatting about their bulls. "Well," said one of them, "myne enter lotter good atorl." "Myne wuz lyke that," said the other, "but I wenter the vet, an' he towld me bowt some stuff I cood git at the chemist ter mearke him moor amerous, an' that dunt harf wakk."

"Woss nearme onnit?" said the first farmer. "Iyll hatter git summer that."

"Carnt member nearme orffhand, but thass inner brown jar an' tearste lyke Marmyte."

A bumper bundle arrived from John Hammond, of Beccles, and I've selected a couple to give you a flavour:

A city chap moved to the country and as he had quite a bit of land at the rear of the house, he bought some little pigs. It wasn't long before the old boy next-door popped his head over the fence saying, "Any advice you want regards them pigs, don't you be afraid to ask."

"Thanks, but I can manage," replied the independent chap.

After a few days, the little pigs looked quite poorly, so the old boy next-door said, "You want to get some pills from the vet for them."

The city chap reluctantly took the advice and went to the vet's, who gave him some little pills to blow into the pig's back passage with the aid of a tube. He went home and caught a little pig by the rear legs, as instructed, inserted the tube but couldn't blow the pill in.

At this point, the old boy, who had been watching the operation, said, "You're making a rare bludder fist of that, boy; let me do that for you." So he took the little pig from the chap, pulled out the tube and stuck it in the other way, blowing in the pill first time.

"Thanks," said the city chap, "but why did you turn the tube round the other way?"

"Well," said the old boy, "I wasn't going to put that in my mouth after you'd been slarvering round it."

A farmer, his wife and eldest son George, went for a week-end holiday, leaving the other son Billy (who was a couple of slates short) to look after the farm. Next day, a neighbouring farmer with his daughter, called at the farm, and said,

"Can I speak to your parents, Billy."

"They gorn away for the week-end," say Billy.

"Well, can I speak to George then."

"No," say Billy. "Cos he's gorn with em, but they've left me in charge, so can I help you."

"Well," said the farmer. "Your brother George has made my daughter pregnant, and I want to know what your father is going to do about it."

"Sorry, but I can't help you," say Billy. "I know how much father charge for the old bull, but I don't know how much he charge for George."

Old friend Ted Beales, of Docking, was in a similar mood:

An elderly maiden lady had a small-holding next to a very large farm. One day she telephoned the farmer asking if she could bring her cow Daisy, to meet his bull. The farmer replied, "You can bring your cow to meet my bull by all means, but I would advise you to ring up the Ministry, and they will send a gentleman along in a bowler hat and he will do the necessary."

She thanked him and in due course rang up the Ministry and was told that a man would be along at 10.30 am next Wednesday, and she must have ready a pail of water, a piece of soap, a towel and of course Daisy the cow.

At 10.30 am the following Wednesday, the man arrived and was told by the old lady, "There's Daisy the cow, there's a pail of water the soap and towel, and I've knocked a nail in the cow house door."

He thanked her, then asked what was the nail for in the cow house door.

She replied, "I thought you'd want somewhere to hang your trousers."

Horses came to the fore in Marjorie Ling's contribution from Carleton Rode:

Some years ago, two farmers met on market day. "George," say Horry. "Wot did yew dew when yar old hoss git the staggers?"

"Whoi ... I give him tarpentyne, bor." George and Horry went their own ways. They met up again next market day.

"George, wot wuz that yew say yew give yar hoss?" "Tarpentine." "Well bor, I dun that – an th'ole hoss died."

"Thass funny, Horry, so did moine!"

Another horse story from Ann Graham, on South Humberside:

A holidaymaker stood at the gate watching the farmer busy in the yard. When the farmer picked up two house-bricks, the visitor asked: "What are you going to do with those?" The farmer replied: "Oim gorter carstreart this hoss. I jest howld a brick in each hand, an' bring mer hands tergether sharpish, an thass dun."

"Goodness, gracious ... doesn't that hurt?"

"Oony if yew git yar thumbs cort atwin the bricks!"

A subtle offering from Syd Rowe, of Sea Palling, concerning a farmer and the young lad late for work:

"Dew yew know wot tyme yew start wakk?"

"Bowt fyve minnit arter I git here."

"No, no ... I meen why are yew learte?"

"Well, thass lyke this here. When that wuz tyme ter cum ter wakk, I wuz asleep. An' I knew that wunt no good a' cummin then ... so I wearted till I wook up."

I culled this one from a local magazine. Ephraim and Willum were working together in the fields, and had been sitting under the hedge having their dinner. When they got up to start work again,

Ephraim felt in his pocket for something, and found he'd lost a shilling. So they started looking for it.

After a while, something Ephraim said made Willum say: "Yew arnt insinireartin Iyre got yar shillin, are yew Ephraim?"

"Oh, no, but Iyre gotter feelin sumhow if yew hent binner helpin me look forrit, I myter fownd it."

Many farmworkers like to show off their talents at the local horticultural show. Jim Neve, of Holme-next-Sea, introduced us to Tom, who'd won most of the prizes as usual. The vicar presented him with his cups, and asked how he always managed to come first.

"Manewer," said Tom. "Good rotten manewer. Orl I ivver ewse is manewer."

Tom went off with his prizes. The vicar turned to the farmworker's wife. "Tom's a marvellous gardener, but I wish you could teach him to call it fertiliser instead of manure."

Tom's wife looked him straight in the collar: "Oill dew moi best, wikker – but thass took me six yeer ter git him ter corl it manewer!"

A tailpiece from John Hammond. During the war, some very young lads from London were evacuees at a Norfolk farm. The farmer had promised to take them to market in the horse and cart.

They waited excitedly by this new form of transport, when one little boy ran into the house shouting: "Come quick, mister, the horse is losing all its petrol!"

Just a few samples of the farmyard humour that says so much about our local character. The stories revived memories, mainly because I heard various versions of some of these jokes – usually with a coarser edge – down on the farm when a sense of humour was of more use to me than a pitchfork.

The first farmyard joke I ever heard has stood the test of time.

Boy to farmer: "Can you use me on the land?"

Farmer to boy: "No . . . weer got speshal stuff fer that!"

CHURCH AND CHAPEL

"Truth from his lips prevailed with double sway,
And folks, who came to scoff, remained to pray"
– Oliver Goldsmith.

Parsons have always been fair game for a laugh. Even bishops can find themselves on the sharp end of Norfolk whimsy. Like the one who'd held a confirmation class in a village, and had stayed overnight with the rector.

He was strolling down the street next day when he came across a group of boys making mud-pies. The bishop saw a number of small mud mountains and asked what they were.

"Pleeze sar, weer playin' confarmearshuns," said one of the lads.

"I see," said the Bishop. "And where, may I ask, is the Bishop?"

"Ah," said the boy, "that tearke a sight o' muck ter mearke a Bishop!"

Ask – and ye shall receive a straight answer. I asked for amusing yarns centred on church or chapel to bring much-needed reverence to the airwaves after weeks of honeycarts, outside toilets and earthy farmyard tales. The collection was impressive.

My Beeston chapel memories were stirred. Preachers who came for tea if they had a double Sunday booking. Mother played the organ, so we were bound to find an extra place at the tea table on occasions.

I don't think we had the local preacher who used to show his gratitude in the pulpit at the evening service. "I would like to thank Mrs Brown for her hospitality."

Mrs Brown, sitting near the front, said loudly: "That wunt horspitality ... that wuz stewed rububb!"

I can reel off the names of so many lay preachers on the Swaffham Methodist Circuit when I was a lad ... Joe Bly, Clar-

• *Harvest Festival echoes at Corpusty.*

Clifford Temple

ence Howlett, Charlie Wilson, E. Wilson, H. J. Harrowing, Harry Ayres, Lorna Bowman, "Happy" Wade, Norman Wagg, Arthur Barrett, Fred Moore, George Read ... to end the list there should not infer I didn't listen to the others!

Sunday school anniversaries, outings to the seaside, carol-singing round the village, Bible examinations, circuit rallies. A full book of memories, with the smiling face and gentle voice of Harry Dawson at the heart of every chapter.

He was our Sunday school teacher, and, by general consent, Beeston's outstanding candidate for a place in Heaven. He told us he was going there one day, and if we really wanted to, we could join him. He treated all children alike, with a calm, amiable tolerance that drew respect and attention.

I can't recall him raising his voice, except for a plaintive "Amen!" at the end of prayers, and he put up with any amount of squit from youngsters because he knew they'd learn to behave themselves in time.

He and his wife Alice were our Sunday mentors for many years, loving characters of the old Methodist school. The simple joy they radiated must have helped scores of Beeston children. The chapel has gone, but the good that some people do lives long after walls have been knocked down.

Harry was a local preacher as well, and that permanent smile told you he liked a good Norfolk yarn. He and his contemporaries used the latest stories doing the rounds to spice up their sermons, and I can remember many yawns being stifled by a sudden shift of emphasis in the pulpit.

The best preachers had a keen sense of humour, and I think the same text can apply to church and chapel today. We often maintain the Devil shouldn't have all the best tunes; nor should he have a monopoly on funny stories.

A story told by a local preacher from the pulpit of North Creake Chapel around 1930 was passed on by the industrious Ted Beales, of Docking:

Three men went out fishing in the

North Sea in a very small rowing boat when a storm blew up. The oars were lost, and the hapless trio were at the mercy of the elements.

One of them cried: "Harry, weer gorter meet owr Mearker by a wortery grearve. Fer Gord's searke, tearke yer hat orff yar hid an' pray forrus ter be searved!"

Harry stood up in the small boat, removed his cap and said after a pause: "Thass no bloomin good, I carnt pray." Turning to the other friend, whose face by now had turned from a healthy pink to a chalky white, he said: "Cum yew on, Arnie, sing us wicket lotter good old hymn."

Arnie stood up, took off his hat, and after a few seconds said: "I carnt sing no hymn – I dunt know wun."

Then the third fisherman stood up and said: "Yewre a nyce lot. Harry coont pray. Arnie dint know no hymn. So I shall hatter dew suffin relijus. Think Iyll tearke the colleckshun."

The inevitable crop from John Hammond, of Beccles. Like the one about the little boy who went to chapel regularly with his mum, who always gave him a shilling to put in the collection.

One Sunday, mum was poorly, so Grandma took him, and when they got to chapel she gave him two bob for the collection. The little boy said loudly: "Wossit gone up this week?"

The old village parson had retired, and the new incumbent was biking round the parish to meet his flock. As he passed the pub, he shouted, "Good morning, gentlemen!" to two old boys sipping their beer on the seat outside.

"Thass owr new parsun," say old George. "Heez a' rummin . . . heer got fyve kids an' nuther wun on the way."

The other old boy took a swig of his pint, wiped away the froth and said drily: "He wotter wear his trowsers searme way he wear his collar."

Another charming vicar story from Jo Ellis, of Swaffham. This vicar had been invited to lunch. The two small sons of the household were tearful, because, in order to feed him in the manner expected, two of the backyard roosters were killed for the occasion.

Silently they sat through the meal while the vicar tucked in. As the family dutifully saw him off, the last of the roosters perched on the garden wall gave a loud "Cockadoodle – doo!"

"My word," said the vicar, "what a proud bird he is!"

One of the little lads, unable to contain himself any longer, blurted out: "An so he shood, Raverend ... heer got tew sons in the Minstry!"

Similar flavour in Henry Suggate's offering from Mutford, near Beccles.

The parson went to the old girl's house, and found her boiling pea soup and bone broth on the hob. He caught a whiff and exclaimed: "How I would love a drop of that, my dear!"

He sat relishing the culinary delights when a little pig came squealing in and kept rubbing against his legs. After a while, he said to Ada: "What a friendly little chap!"

Ada looked at him. "Yis, he know yew're got his bearsin."

Harold Lock of the Fish Shop at East Harling, served up the one about Billy and Jimmy having a mardle while leaning on the church wall overlooking the graveyard.

"Jimma, where wood yew lyke ter lay when the tyme cum?"

"Hent thowt much bowt it, but sinse yew arsk, I woont mynd layin in that corner nexter owld Charlie Smith. He wuz a good farmer, an' rekun weed git on orrite tergether. Wot bowt yew? Where wood yew lyke ter lay?"

"Long syder Patsy Walker unner that yew tree."

"Howld yar row ... she ent ded yit."

"I know thet ... an' nor arnt I!"

A bit of licence, I suppose, and Dave Scott, of Norwich, wasn't too bothered about the rules when he put pen to paper.

A chap left the pub after a good session,

wandered into the church and into the confessional. The priest on the other side heard someone come in, and then ... nothing.

After about five minutes, he decided to attract the attention of the person on the sinner's side. So he knocked on the partition. The drunk spoke.

"Thash no good knockin', ole mearte, theer ent ner pearper in thish wun either!"

And I thought we'd got clean away from that sort of humour. To help redress the balance, I turned to a few examples from *More Norfolk Tales and Memories*, by B. Knyvet Wilson, first published in 1931.

A new parson had arrived in the village. (Thank goodness they keep on the move to keep the stories flowing.) The wife of a small farmer said to her boy: "Now then, John, I want yew ter run downter the ractory an tearke that new raverind harfer pownd o' my butter. Happen heel lyke that, an that mite leed ter bizness."

John duly delivered the butter, and said to the new parson: "My mar, she sent yew this heer butter as a prasent lyke." The parson replied; "What beautiful butter! And how does your mother do all that fancy scrollwork on top, my lad?"

The boy looked up. "Ooh, that ent harf eezy. She dew that wi' owr coomb!"

The Norfolk flair for getting words slightly mixed up is given full rein in this one. "Let me see," said a visitor to the old parish clerk. "Do you have mattins now in this church?"

"No, sar, no ... not now we dunt. We hev a linoleum rite up the whool way as far's the alter!"

There's plenty of honest country logic in the tale of the parson who was anxious to entice the local mole-catcher to church. He tried him with a few roundabout questions, to all of which the old boy returned "fencing" replies.

Eventually, the parson said: "I am sorry to say I have not worshipped in the same building with you lately, Sam."

The old boy gave the parson an old-fashioned look and said: "Dunt yew know, sar, as yew shunt nivver set a trap fer the searme moll in the searme plearse twice!"

Fred Wigby, that famous son of Wicklewood, and Radio Norfolk's "Grand Old Mardler", chipped in with the story of the two old locals discussing the collection being made to raise money for new church gates.

"Dunno why they bother," said Caleb. "Them woss in theer carnt git owt – an us woss owt heer dunt pertickely wotter go in."

Before we give this chapter our blessing, let me commend two more items, one a more subtle snippit that ought to be true, and the other a shining example of Norfolk invention.

A country parson was invited to dine with the squire. He dined and wined well, and in the early hours of the next day he made his way home. Later on, the squire's man brought a message.

"My master says if you will return his bird cage, he will let you have your lantern."

Verse 105 from the longest Psalm of them all, Psalm 119, may sum that one up best: "Thy word is a lamp unto my feet, and a light unto my path."

But I'll praise all parsons and preachers with a sense of humour with a highly-individual version of the Lord's Prayer, sent in by Allan Thompson, of Poringland:

In the church, the corncrake-ation bow their heads as the vicar says: "We will now say the Lark's Preyer. Let osprey – Owl feather, whinchat in heron, mallard be thy crane, thy ringdove cock, thy whimbrel dunlin eider as ibis in heron: mavis this jay our jayly grebe, and forgive us our treecreepers as we forgive wren that treecreep mergansers; and linnets knot into ternation, but teal-dipper us from eagle, for thine is the ringdove, the plover and the dodo, for-ruffer,

Moorhen."

That was delivered by carrier pigeon with the suggestion: "This ought to curlew up."

• *Cranking-up a faithful old-timer.*

Clifford Temple

MEDICAL MATTERS

"Life is made up of sobs, sniffles, and smiles, with sniffles predominating"
– O. Henry.

It was obvious by now that listeners could wring laughs from any subject, so I had no qualms about asking for amusing stories from "Bedpan Alley".

Going into hospital, especially for the first time, is a traumatic experience, but there's still a rich thread of humour running through life on the wards. Many lasting friendships are forged, while gratitude to doctors and nurses is as sincere as it is predictable.

I had my tonsils out at the Norfolk and Norwich Hospital a few years ago, and, in between serious bouts of cowardice and shame that others with worse afflictions weren't showing themselves up, I caught a whiff of that special comradeship.

One patient who'd undergone a rather delicate operation insisted on giving us lurid details at breakfast time – and it doesn't take much to put me off my cornflakes. Another kept his mum's tasty doughnuts for our midnight feast and cabaret, which brought mild complaints from the women's ward next door. (They'd not been invited.)

Top prize for style went to the chap who kissed his wife goodbye, and then prepared himself for a visit from one of his old flames. He had to own up after puckering his lips for the second time within an hour. A no-nonsense nurse denied him a hat-trick, but he knew he wouldn't be quite as attractive after his nose operation.

"Laughter is the best medicine" was a constant theme of letters recalling hospital escapades. Eileen Foulger, of Shotesham, had her moments at the Norfolk and Norwich:

"It was just coming up to lunchtime, and I was wondering what would be on the menu. I also thought I'd better pay a visit to the loo before the trolley came round.

"It was a bit of a shock when I saw this bedpan on the floor, covered and with the word 'Dinner' written on a piece of paper. I could see the funny side of this, and when I went back to the ward, I discovered that the lady in the next bed to me was a Mrs Dinner, and they'd been taking specimens to prepare her for her operation that afternoon."

Eileen and Mrs Dinner became close friends.

In 1980, Harry Smith, of Norwich, had his right kidney removed. "I had no food for 36 hours. And what do you think my first meal was? Yes . . . kidney soup, which for some reason I didn't really fancy!"

Rachel Cooper, of Roughton, near Cromer, wasn't a model patient when she went in to have her second son. "First, I was in a ward with Pat Medler, from Aylsham, and we giggled so much we had to be separated like naughty schoolgirls for keeping the other patients awake.

"Then Ann moved in with me, and I said I'd get her a jar of honey, which I duly did and placed it on her bed table. She thought she'd picked it up, but didn't quite make it – and it smashed on the floor, covering a very large area with sticky, liquid honey.

"I think they were glad to get rid of me at the end of ten days – little knowing they'd have me back 18 months later for the third boy!"

Christine Kett, of Norwich, was a nurse in the early 1960s, and her hospital dished up two types of meal "take it or leave it." At most mealtimes there were moans and groans, so I used to joke with the men and say, 'Come on, eat up . . . it'll put hairs on your chest!'

"When I moved on to the female surgical ward, up came the moans for my first mealtime there. Forgetting which ward I was on, I gave the patients my usual inducement. A dear old soul with a high-pitched, haughty voice piped up: 'Nurse, I don't think we require hairs on our chests after the operations we have had!'"

Nearly fifty years ago, Mabel Brown, of Dereham, was a night nurse in a Yorkshire hospital. She called the patients one morning at six with a cup of tea and a cheerful greeting. One patient said, "Nurse you remind me of a Spring morning." Mabel asked why. "Because you are soft and balmy!" Ward alive with laughter. A real tonic to start the day.

From there to maternity ... When she was in Drayton Hall, near Norwich, a few years back, Mary Hammond, of Whinburgh, near Dereham, remembered the girl in the next bed was a Catholic, and had just had her fifth baby.

"The local rector called, and said he'd better tell us of a new kind of birth control. 'Each night, take a glass of water to bed. Don't take it before. Don't take it after. But instead of.' It must work. Mary hasn't been back to Drayton yet."

My winning letter in the "Bedpan Alley" file came from Bebe Newman, of Great Yarmouth. It's worth the full treatment:

"After being involved in an accident, I came round to find myself in hospital, very uncomfortable, strung up in traction with a fractured neck of the femur.

"A few days later, a couple of nurses came to me and said they wanted to turn me so they could get at my back to treat it and prevent any soreness developing. So, with a lot of struggling on their part, and a lot of 'oh, oh's' on mine, it was accomplished – only for them both to collapse in hysterical laughter.

"Next minute, along comes the ward sister, who could have been Peggy Mount's twin. She gave one look, and joined in. She came round to the head of the bed, and in her open palm were a pair of earrings.

"I'd forgotten I was wearing them on the day of the accident. I suppose, being so uncomfortable and restless, I must have pushed them out of my ears – and they'd made their way down the bed, ending up well and truly embedded, one in each cheek!

• *January ploughing at Acle – and no furrowed brows.*

Clifford Temple

"The sister said, 'Well, I've seen some remarkably handsome backsides in my time, but this is the first one studded with diamonds!'

"I always knew I was a cut above the rest of the family," said Bebe. What an absolute gem of a story with which to draw the curtains on "Bedpan Alley".

I was thinking out loud one day during the programme – an occupational hazard for which there is little therapy – about a certain matter that had been worrying me for some time.

Why do men have fluff in their belly-button, while women, as far as I'm aware, do not? An intriguing poser, but I wasn't expecting such an avalanche of useful information in my search for an answer.

"Doctor" Kath Bygrave gave the subject top priority with this diagnosis:

"The irritating complaint, Fluff in the belly-button, (or, 'Lintus Navellus', as we doctors call it), is caused by the wearing of old, disintegrating cotton pants or woollen long johns, and the reason that women do not suffer from this affliction is because they wear nylon briefs, (if anything), manufactured from material which does not shed 'lints' or 'fluff'.

"The accumulated deposits of debris should be removed carefully with the pointed end of a nail-file, sterilised letter-opener, or pair of eyebrow-tweezers, by the sufferer, if the navel is visible to him, or by a friend if the sufferer is too obese to obtain a clear view of the operation area himself.

"The old-fashioned underwear should be replaced by a pair of those tastefully pictorially-decorated modern briefs, and the condition will not recur, though, unfortunately, it may well be replaced, in the case of sensitive individuals, by the equally irritating skin complaint, 'Radio Presenter's Bum' (or, as we doctors call it), 'Dermatitus Bottus' – a purple rash on the parts that the air cannot reach, due to the non-absorbent properties of nylon, and relief from *this* distressing condition necessitates frequent exposure of the affected parts of the light of a full moon (or, as we doctors say, the 'Maximus Luminus Lunaticus' treatment), on the homeopathic principle that like cures like."

Sound advice followed from a most unlikely source:

"Illustrious One!

"Excuse, please, but in my country, where many common people squat, cross-legged in the gutters, all day, wearing nothing but a dirty dhoti, making most wondrous rugs for the English Gentry in many Heavenly Colours, fluff in the belly-button is a very common thing.

"Fortunately, Allah, in his wisdom, has provided for this most unhappy condition by creating a small insect called a Carpet Mite. He takes up his residence in the male belly-button, and devours all kinds and colours of fluff most ravenously.

"Our female women are also engaged in the fabrication of these wondrous carpets from the age of three years, but their habit of wearing a Precious Jewel in the belly-button prevents the accumulation of fluff therein.

"If you would please to search diligently in the belly-buttons of your female women colleagues you may find they also have some device to prevent this most unfortunate affliction!

Your most affectionately,
I. Mustapha Feel, M.D.,
(Prof., Univ. of Cairo)."

Boy John told the quack, "I've brook out
In a rash." So the Doc had a snout.
"Drop 'em down!" said the quack,
"Legs apart! Bend yar back!
Ah, thass suffin woss gorn about!"

Kath Bygrave (Hethersett)

Tina Little, of Necton, put her thoughts in verse:

Fluff in Men's Navels

My heart, old beauty, you set us a task
When this personal question of us you
  ask.
Why in men's buttons is there more fluff
Than in those belonging to bits of stuff?

I put the question to the men in my
  house
Including the dog, the cat and the mouse.
But they could not give the reason why,
So they're no help to you or I.

I then shut myself away in the study
And read all the books on the human
  body.
No references to buttons could I find,
So then I had to search my mind.

Well, after some thought I'd like to
  suggest
That the fluff that accumulates comes
  from the vest.
And the reason why it stays in there
Is because it's probably trapped with
  hair.

Because most men's stomachs are so
  stout
The button is angled so fluff can't drop
  out.
And in closing, I'd like to say . . .
Who asked you this question anyway?

Mind you, I could have asked the wife in the privacy of our own consulting room. She tells me nature intended it that way. So women have shelves to prevent the fluff from getting as far as the belly-button.

• *Windmill at Thornham Parva surveys the fields.*

Clifford Temple

ASSORTED SMILES

"He who laughs last — probably didn't get the joke in the first place"

– Norfolk wag.

With humour very much the keynote of these pages, I've had to shelve hundreds of other letters for the time being, mainly because they deal with more serious subjects. Those letters may provide scope for another Norfolk-based volume at a later date.

The study of literature written in our local dialect is just one of the other areas of close inspection, and I'm happy to include short stories, verses and pages of memories from Dinnertime listeners in that exercise.

After all, dialect, thankfully, is not a matter for reflection, but still a proudly fluttering flag of parochialism, a living part of everyday language for many Norfolk people.

We can use it to amuse or welcome the newcomer; we can wear it as armour against the armies of "progress"; we still employ it as a weapon of laughter, often at our own expense, and as a subtle means of getting away with stories that would have to be labelled offensive if delivered in orthodox language.

Norfolk isn't the only place with respect and affection for its dialect, but in common with those other areas which value their sense of individuality, we must confront outside influences with unstinting faith in our survival programme.

I contend that the best way of preserving dialect is to use it, even if a self-conscious edge creeps in at times. Jonathan Mardle confessed to being uncomfortable when people organised competitions to prove it was still alive. There was a danger, he thought, it would become more of an affectation than a genuine hymn of praise.

Frankly, I don't think it matters at a time when people and places are being urged to become boring photostats of everyone and everywhere else. Uniformity is dull, and any attempt to pick holes in the pattern should be applauded.

Like the dialect evening that's become a proud tradition at the Cromer and North Norfolk Festival of Music and Drama.

I've been heartened by the number of letters sent to me in the local dialect, and not always from listeners who've been brought up with it. Several newcomers to the area have waded in bravely, especially on the less-demanding limerick front, and I'm not being patronising when I dish out compliments and encouraging marks for probing the mysteries of a foreign tongue.

Ron Graves, of Mundford, didn't have any problems getting his Norfolk tale over with the full flavour when I asked for local cricket stories. Ron came to the crease with this epic passed on by Tony Curry, of Bodney:

"They ewsed ter play cricket on the park at Hillborough, an theer wuz a gret ole tree near the pitch. One day, ol' Joe hit the borl, an blarst me if that din't lodge up the tree. The batsmin kept a' runnin, an when they hed run six, the uther team say ter the umpire, 'Thassa lorst borl, an they carnt run ner moor'n six.'

"'How kin that be a lorst borl,' say the umpire, 'when I kin see it latched up that theer tree?' So the batsmin kep a' runnin while sumwun hossed over to the Hall to git a ladder. By the time he git back, they had run a hundred an twetty-three afore he git the borl down. Then they hed ter hoss orff back ter the Hall ter git sum brandy for the batsmin who wuz orl of a muckwosh an propply dorzled."

A grand sporting moment captured forever, simply because Ron Graves listened and wrote it down. Clearly, his years as a local press correspondent made it a labour of love.

Geoff Hall, of Gressenhall, remembered something his dad told him, a little idea as to what should be depicted on the Norfolk

Coat of Arms: "A raggetty-arsed littel archin with a snotty snowt eatin a swede tannip on a frosty mornin'!" You don't forget descriptions like that.

Henry Suggate, of Mutford, near Beccles, demanded attention with his bits of squit: "I hatter tell yer bowt my bruther Charley. He wuz bykin long uther day with a short ladda on his showda, when ole Fred hallered owt over his gearte: 'Wot are yew now gorter dig a hool, Charley?' 'No,' he say, 'Oim jest a'gorn ter gather a few windforls.' We ewsed ter hev a blook in the willuj an his nearme wuz Fred, so we corled him 'Austrearlia' fer short...." Sound local logic.

Don Lusha, of Tittleshall, pushed forward a friend who went to Great Yarmouth Races one day. After the last race, he saw a cockle and whelk stall parked near the exit. Being a great lover of shellfish, he bought the largest whelk he'd ever seen. It took him five minutes to chew and eventually swallow.

The stallholder gave him a huge grin: "Cor blarst, yewre dun well, ole partner – three blooks hedder go at that wun orridy!"

Although he was born in Norfolk, John Hylton, of Tharston, doesn't have a strong local accent: "A few years ago when visiting a farmhouse in the next village, I was asked in for a cup of tea. Waiting on my own in the living room, I could hear the signs of preparation – cups, saucers and spoons clinking, and then the sound of the kettle boiling.

"The door squeaked open and in walked the big and friendly farm dog. He sat down by my chair and pushed his cold, wet nose into my hand, his eyes begging me to coax him. I stroked the smooth, silky head, saying, 'Good boy! Good boy!'

"A voice from the kitchen called out, 'But I've made the tea. I thought you could stop ... must you really go?' I was completely bewildered. Then I answered, 'I'm not going. What made you think that?'

"'Well', she said. 'You said "Good Boi!"' It all became clear, and I explained to the farmer's wife how we had got confused. 'My hat!' she exclaimed. 'You must think I'm a rummen!'"

There are plenty of examples of unintentionally funny notes being sent to schoolteachers from Norfolk parents. Like the mother whose boy was suffering from constipation: "Johnny carnt go, but arter heer bin heel cum."

Gwen Cooper, of Hempnall, was reminded of the little notes her father used to find pinned on people's doors when they were out as he delivered their groceries.

From a customer who went out to "do" for the local gentry: "Dear Mr Stammers. I may not see you on Tuesday as I have to go to my ladies."

From an old lady who had to go up the city on the bus: "Dear Mr Stammers, cannot see you today as I have to go up the hospital with my eyes, and I have to be sure to be there with them at three o'clock."

And a note left for Gwen's aunt, Miss Alice Stammers, who helped with the delivery rounds during the war: "Dear Miss Stammers. Sorry not to leave you any money today, but my mother dying put me in a hole."

An amorous cleric from Docking
Met a lady whose morals were shocking.
An encounter which led,
As the newspapers said,
To a case of a double unfrocking.

Geoff Ashworth (Marsham)

Now for a couple of poetic efforts that gave me so much pleasure as the squit bandwagon rolled on. The first was inspired by Radio Norfolk's "Night of Squit" at Cromer Pier in June, 1984, when local artists gloried in the vernacular. Jill Mason, of Castleacre, put it like this:

NORFOLK SQUIT

I'm an immigrant from Sussex
And I've moved here with my kit.
But my dictionary's bloody useless
For deciphering Norfolk squit.

I even went to Cromer Pier
To learn some translations
From Benton, Crisp and Skipper
and "Muck Carter's" recitations.

On Saturday trips to Swaffham
To the market on the stones
My old man interprets
The locals' lilting tones.

Hearing the Norfolk dialect
Is a pleasure that I likes
As I wander round the ducks and goats,
The furniture and bikes.

Down South, the Sussex lingo
It's been fashionable to quash
By teachers and by parents
Who made us speak right posh.

Moving here to Norfolk's
Like walking back in life,
No high-powered business pressures,
None of the rat-race life.

Norfolk folk know where they stand,
They think in black and white
They don't try keeping up with Jones,
But keep up the pub each night.

Their humour's somewhat earthy
To say the least of it.
They tell of daily happenings,
Saying it's a load of squit.

They have a knack of stating
What is obvious and clear
In words that are so simple
As they down a pint of beer.

My pa-in-law knows lots of tales
I'd copy as he tells 'em,
But when I come to write the words
I don't know how you spells 'em.

So cherish your Norfolk dialect,
Your mardlin' and your squit,
For life would be less colourful
If you were minus it.

An unsolicited testimonial from a newcomer to Norfolk.

Teenager Anne Plummer, of Great Cressingham, sent a poem she'd written at school. "We were doing a lesson on dialects, and we had to pick one and write a poem. I chose the Norfolk dialect because I'd spent all my 15 years at Great Cressingham. . . .

"ORL 'BOUT NORFIK"

Oi loike a-livin' in Norfik
tha's a verry noice plairce t'be,
thar in't roight a lot gorn on, thow
but that don't matters t' me!

Yew c'n see th' owd harnsers on the
 Brords,
An' th' dodmans in th' grass,
Hev a grairt ol' plairt o' sanfer,
an' wotch the boots go past.

Gorn spend a dare in Norrich,
or walk up th' golden moile,
even tairk a trip t' Hunst'n,
attle orl be wath y' woile!

Ha yew tearsted Norfik Dumplun's
cooked in less than half 'n' hour?
They wholly blow y' belly up,
an' there only meard a' flar!

Oi spoose ya heard o' Wayland Wood
tha's nawn f' near 'n' far,
I read the book 'bout the bearbs
'n' that wholly maird me blar!

Tha's only sum o' Norfik,
Thars a lot that oi hent sin,
but if yew cum this way, bore
I bet you're glad your bin!

"Wotcher Joe, me old pal, howyer diddlin?"
Said George. Joe replied, "Fair ter middlin,
But fed up with this mud,
Can't lift beet ner yit spud,
I'll be glad when this rearn's stopped a' piddlin."

Ivy West (Corpusty)

On the troshel stood pasty-faced Dick.
Said the dentist, "You're lookin' quite sick."
When he saw Dick's large molar,
He said, "Cor! What a soler!
I'd best use a shovel and pick."

Margaret Loose (Blakeney)

• *Bodham's "Killmagrannie Pipe Band" in full cry at the village's notorious "Night of Squit".*

SQUIT MERCHANTS

"Life is a jest; and all things show it.
I thought so once; but now I know it"
– John Gay.

There are plenty of squit merchants in Norfolk. Many of them are natural purveyors, nudging, winking, yarning and chuckling down the village pub every night.

The audience are usually the same, egging on performers to break into well-worn routines, often packed with local references that vary from the amiable jibe to the blunt insult.

They're fairly safe on home ground, and the relaxed climate of the pub stage has encouraged several memorable bouts of banter. It's a delight to watch and listen to a couple of village wags exchange points of view, build up to a crescendo of mutual scorn that would do the House of Commons justice – and then buy each other a half!

Squit in the raw. Impromptu trading in verbal blows. Disagreeing for the sheer hell of it. Seeking support from an unsuspecting stranger. Tearing off your jacket in mock anger. And then pretending you'll get told off "suffin wicked" when you get home late. (The best pub squit merchants melt away while the laughter's still bubbling.)

Of course, such invigorating nonsense can flourish in other areas, like the village hall. That's where I've savoured countless examples on my rural rides of recent years.

From Bodham to Bradenham, Hevingham to Horning, Garvestone to Ovington, East Tuddenham to Walsingham, Thornham to Yaxham, Kenninghall to Swardeston ... and many others where the yarns have flowed and the friendships blossomed.

It may be the chap on the microphone spicing up the raffle draw; the mawther

Loading-up at Ludham – and shades of the past.

Clifford Temple

lured into the spotlight to give 'em a song at the end of the social evening; the committee member bribed into telling the only local joke fit for the parson's ears: the parson going one better.

Spontaneous fun feeding the community spirit, with relative newcomers – in the village for less than 20 years – making their pitch as the mood mellows.

Bodham, near Holt, has an enviable reputation for homegrown indulgence in the shape of their annual "Night of Squit", held in March to give locals the chance to get over Christmas.

They've gone right to the top in a bid to apportion blame for this rural eisteddfod. "I suppose it must be Her Majesty The Queen," said Mik Godfrey, one of the Bodham impressarios behind the extravaganza. "After all, if she hadn't celebrated her Silver Jubilee in 1977, it would possibly have never started."

Word went out that a variety concert was to be staged in the village hall as part of the Jubilee celebrations, with locals soon press-ganged into doing a turn. A one-off session has turned into an annual event, with everything from dancing girls to outrageous sketches – and handsome helpings of earthy Norfolk humour.

To give proceedings that off-the-cuff touch, those taking part organise their own items independently. So, until the show is presented before a noisy, expectant audience, nobody really knows what's likely to happen.

I've completed a hat-trick in the "Night of Squit" attendance book. Happily, it shows no sign of getting any better.

Mik Godfrey's sparring partner in the spotlight, introducing the acts if they're ready, is Barry Toyn. They're delighted that lack of shame is a ready commodity at Bodham. On the first night – yes, they have the cheek to do it twice – the running order is pinned up backstage. It's probably been amended three or four times to cater for last-minute additions or cancellations. (The pub next door could have something to do with that.)

The week-end before curtain-up, trestles and boards that make up the stage are brought down from their storage space above the kitchen in the hall. Hammering and hollering. Curtains rcpaired.

A small gap's left behind the stage where the crew can assemble during the show. The kitchen is the communal changing room. Chaos is predictable. Props, costumes, bottles of "Dutch Courage", and a spaghetti of wires leading to microphones and amplifiers. Little things go wrong. Taped music refuses to start. Someone trips over a wire and pulls the plug out. Betty Earnshaw forgets to close the curtains. Ruddy Sparks is missing. It all helps to maintain the Bodham reputation.

When the "Killmagrannie Pipe Band" were in full cry in 1979, Robert Wright made his mark in spectacular fashion during a display of counter-marching. He took one pace too many in a backward direction and fell straight off the back of the stage. He clambered back, bloody, but unbowed, and finished the performance. Luckily, there wasn't a microphone backstage at the time ... as his remarks were more Anglo-Saxon than Scottish.

"It's not the greatest show on earth," said Mik Godfrey. "We don't want it to be. As long as we enjoy making fools of ourselves, and the audience enjoy watching us do it, we've achieved our objective of keeping alive the old community spirit in one small Norfolk village.

"Perhaps the secret of our excess is that we're endowed with an above-average number of village idiots. . . ."

The village hall is half-a-century old, and they're busy raising money to build a new one at Bodham. Raising so many laughs is certainly helping that cause. You wouldn't believe it to see them chortling, singing and clapping, but the Bodham folk are fully capable of getting their danders up. They made one hell of a fuss when the village school was threatened with closure. It's still open.

"This is a funny village, with just as

many awkward beggars here as anywhere else. But when they want something done, and they think it's worth doing, they all muck in and get busy – and that includes many of the newcomers," I was told in the Red Hart pub next door after the most recent "Night of Squit".

Bodham is twinned with Ovington, near Watton, and a free exchange of ideas and visits has inspired both communities to try new schemes. Norfolk's first village twinning was launched at Ovington in December, 1984, on a clear, frosty night as the local entertainers changed in a tent behind the small village hall.

Not that Bodham's buccaneers of mirth have forgotten their duties closer to home. East and West Beckham up the road join in the frivolities. It's a bit like big brothers and sisters letting the little 'uns dress up and go to the dance. "They ent got noffin theer, so we sorter look arter 'em."

Rural teamwork to keep the squit flowing. Finally, in this celebration of Norfolk's most alluring characteristic, a solo turn from the man who, in my book, has demonstrated in the last decade how local humour can be elevated to an art form.

David "Muck Carter" Lambert, in rustic outfit to match his droll delivery, has been compared with Sidney Grapes, "The Boy John", who enjoyed local fame for many years as a dialect comedian before he wrote his first letter and introduced all those memorable characters to readers of the *Eastern Daily Press*.

I never saw Sidney Grapes on the concert platform, but I gather he gloried to the full in the role of the rustic who wasn't such a fool as he looked. The audience would be laughing at him halfway through a yarn, but by the time he'd got to the punchline, they were laughing with him.

That's been very much the format enjoyed by "Muck Carter", daring his listeners to get there first, and then milking the moment as they finish together in a gale of laughter.

• *David "Muck Carter" Lambert taking the mike.*

"The Boy John" ran a garage at Potter Heigham. "Muck Carter" has a boot and shoe repairs shop at Attleborough. Clear indications there of using natural comic gifts as no more than a hobby, mainly because Norfolk dialect exponents accept the limitations of their native tongue. It doesn't travel well – although there have been efforts to "educate" a wider audience.

The BBC, perhaps foreseeing the advent of local wireless stations, gave "The Boy John" a bigger stage, and he took great glee in recalling how he once broadcast a joke with ribald undertones. It was so carefully wrapped it slipped through the censors' net!

A couple of years ago, when BBC Radio 4 asked me to host an East Anglian celebration called "Wotcher Bor!" from the Sparrow's Nest Theatre at Lowestoft, "Muck Carter" was the automatic choice to dispense earthy humour in the local idiom.

He was assured of a warm reception from the natives, many of whom had savoured his menu before, but my lasting memory is of technicians from the capital holding their sides and tripping over microphone wires (just like Bodham) as they caught the gist of his offerings.

A heartening breakthrough, but "Muck Carter" shrugged off suggestions that he should graduate to "missionary" work in the capital or elsewhere.

I suggest Norfolk comedians will always be happier on their own midden, accepting that any dilution or compromise outside will be an insult to the genuine article.

That in itself is the beauty of our squit – it begs no cheap imitators. How often we've cringed at network television and radio attempts to portray Norfolk dialect and idiosyncracies! The abolition of "Mummerzet" must remain top priority for our cultural mentors in the big cities.

David "Muck Carter" Lambert, sadly, has retired from the local comedy circuit, except for a few bookings he's determined to honour. His business is flourishing, and he'll be glad of a few Saturday nights at home with his wife Mary, herself a dab hand when it comes to home-made entertainment.

So, as "Muck Carter's" reign as successor to "The Boy John" passes into Norfolk lore – and I guarantee most of his yarns will stay in circulation – it's worth plotting his course to the squit peerage.

A shy, modest man, in such sharp contrast to the "Jack The Lad" comics so abundant on the national scene with their machine-gun volleys of one-liners, he was born at Barningham Winter on St David's Day (March 1st) in 1936. David was one of eight children, and his father was a farmworker.

On leaving school, he got a job reboring engines. That lasted a fortnight, and he was then taken on by a Holt cobbler as an apprentice.

Called up for National Service, he thought there'd be a chance to do something different. He spent the whole two years mending army boots.

Back in civvy street, and still very much the country boy, he went to work as a shoe repairer in Wymondham. (Travel is good for the sole.)

His introduction to showbusiness was hardly glamorous. Brother Geoffrey formed "The Wayfinders", based in Horsford, and they went round the county, mostly entertaining old people. David made a comic cat, with various gadgets to make its eyes swivel and light up. While another member of the concert party did an act, David sat at the back of the hall working the controls. It wasn't a purring success, and David started to do a little turn of his own.

Wedding bells beckoned for David and Mary. "The Wayfinders" broke up. The cat was redundant. But "Muck Carter" – the name was donated by his brother – gradually came out of his shell as he took a job in the trim shop at Lotus Cars.

Opportunity knocked at Christmas time when anyone with a modicum of talent had to get up and do their thing. "Muck Carter" was a hit, and invited to appear at the firm's festive party.

Later that year, when a local contest was organised, one of "Muck Carter's" colleagues was entered. He was very nervous. "Dunt worry boy, if you win this week, I'll enter next." He did win – and Master Lambert went sailing through all the heats except the last. "We had a lovely year," said Mary. "He won lots of whisky, going from Wymondham to Diss, Clacton and Canvey Island."

The bookings came in. The "Muck Carter" squit wagon was on its way for over a decade. He never advertised for work, but he was always in demand. He much preferred to entertain a pensioners' club rather than head for the holiday camps on the coast. There were automatic problems with the Scots: they didn't understand a word he was saying!

Much more at home on the rural beat, he helped raise thousands of pounds for village halls. Ilketshall St Lawrence was a favourite, but the relationship had uneasy beginnings. Mary painted the picture:

"A few years ago, I had a call from a Mrs Webb, who'd been given David's phone number. She said, 'I'm on my knees. I'm trying to build some new toilets at our village hall. But I've been let down by someone who was coming to entertain us at our Harvest Supper. Can your husband help?'

"David said he'd go over, and they had a smashing night. For about five years after that, we'd both go, and David would do his turn. We became firm friends with the Webbs. But Mrs Webb told me later that when she saw David come in the door for that first booking, she thought, 'My God! What have I done!' She didn't think David was capable of putting on an act, let alone make them laugh."

Not such a fool as he looked. A true Norfolk character who cobbled together a memorable act out of what he'd heard and seen around him. Some of the stories, ready-made for the slow-burn style, were green with age when he got hold of them. But the impeccably droll presentation ensured another long innings.

Norfolk's special brand of humour hasn't been exclusively in the hands and hearts of "The Boy John" and "Muck Carter" for the past half-century. Even so, it's easy to crown them the natural kings of squit during that time. It's a sincere hope that some who fell under the rustic spell will be inspired to carry on the tradition.

Taking a cue from Aunt Agatha, that wise dispenser of homely truths, I'll accept that "the more yow say, the less people remember", and leave you with my favourite story from the "Muck Carter" handbook of humour. It's pure squit:

A village lad was making his first visit after dark to the big city of Norwich. He was fascinated by all the sights, especially the castle in all its illuminated glory. As he stood gaping, a lady of the night edged towards him in her high heels and fur coat.

She didn't get any reaction as she clicked her heels on the pavement, so she tugged his overalls and whispered: "Dew yew wotter bit?"

His eyes still aloft, he replied: "Whoi? Watter they gorter knock it down?"

When the bride of a cowman called Fred
Found him wearing his breeches in bed,
He explained, to her horror,
"That searve toime termorrer.
Rownd hair we dew different!" he said.

Kath Bygrave (Hethersett)

When this bobby on duty went forth,
You knew he was from Norfolk (North),
He didn't bend at the knees,
And say "Move along please",
He said, "Cleer yew orff,
Cleer yew orff,
Cleer yew orff!"

H. E. Glaister (Brandon)

ACKNOWLEDGEMENTS

In compiling this load of Norfolk squit, I've been delighted to receive help and encouragement from so many fellow-enthusiasts. My first bouquet must go to BBC Radio Norfolk Dinnertime Show listeners, who provided the raw material in the shape of letters, limericks and memories. It seemed natural to give them a more permanent airing in a volume dedicated to Norfolk's sense of humour. I'm indebted to Major Egbert Gladstone-Pyle for his learned yet friendly foreword penned at Wanglingham Hall. He leaves his country seat to dispense aristocratic truths on my programme, but he accepts there can be no class barriers when it comes to appreciating true squit. Other Dinnertime Show contributors were eager to give support. Thanks to "Dumpling Donna" Clarke, of Brampton, for her pictorial safari in search of the privy down the yard, and to Mik Godfrey for his kind assistance in unravelling the mysteries of Bodham's Night of Squit. Mary Lambert built the stage for husband "Muck Carter" to raise all those laughs on the comedy circuit. Entertainer Bobby Benton allowed me to give his Honeycart Song my own written treatment.

Several supporters were quick to give permission to use their photographs, including Clifford Temple, of Norwich, whose Norfolk collection is as big as it is impressive. (Buy his books and see what I mean!) Litcham friends have been particularly helpful, and I thank Ron Shaw, of the Litcham Historical Society, and Peter Rowe for the splendid picture on the front cover of Wally Feeke and his famous honeycart. On the back, the Lound honeycart is doing the rounds in the snow, thanks to Mr H. Harwood, of Great Yarmouth.

To all others who've contributed in any way, my warmest gratitude – and may they long continue to savour the glories of Norfolk squit.

Keith Skipper.

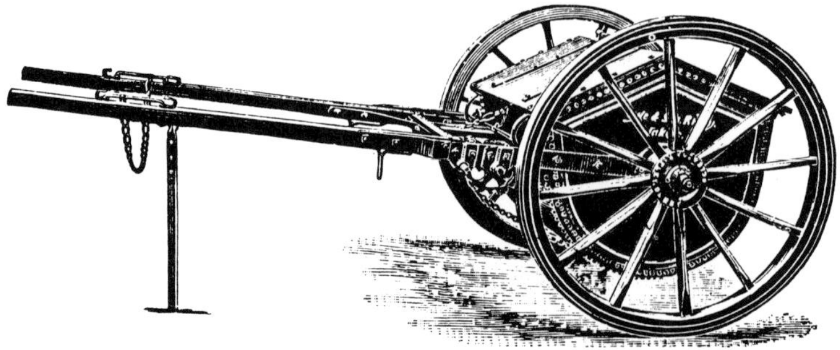